10/06

WITHDRAWN

D0858891

A PLEDGE TO THE SUFFERING

"For each copy of this edition purchased through the website, FadingTowardEnlightenment.com, I will donate $5.00 to the charity of the customer's choice." - Wayne Wirs

Seekers ARE different.
Buy a book.
Tell a friend.
Ease the suffering.

Please go to FadingTowardEnlightenment.com for a list of charities supported by this program.

FADING TOWARD
ENLIGHTENMENT

Life between the Ego and the Ethereal

Photography and Text by
WAYNE WIRS

Missing Man Press

St. Louis Community College
at Meramec
LIBRARY

Missing Man Press
http://missingmanpress.com

Copyright © 2005 by Wayne Wirs

All rights reserved. No part of this book may be reproduced in
any form or by any means, electronic or mechanical, including
photocopying, recording, or by any informational storage and
retrieval system, without permission in writing from the publisher.

First Edition
Printed in the United States of America

Edited by Mary Liu.
Cover and Interior Design by Wayne Wirs.
All photographs by Wayne Wirs.

ISBN: 0-9763581-0-7
Library of Congress Control Number: 2004116607

Notice of disclaimer: The information and suggestions provided
in this book are based on the experiences and opinions of the
author. The author and publisher will not be responsible or liable
for the use or misuse of the information in this book.

DEDICATION

F*ading Toward Enlightenment* is dedicated to all the Spiritual Seekers who, in their quest for Inner Peace, sacrifice some of their Normality, to recognize some of their Divinity.

You may be different – but you are not alone.

The ideal is in thyself, the impediment too is in thyself

Thomas Carlyle

PREFACE

Yearning. Hope. Promise. Salvation.
These are the words of the spiritual seeker, of the dissatisfied and the distraught — these are the words that motivate the Hero to rise up and venture forth to lands distant and unknown.

Yearning. Hope. Promise. Salvation.
Powerful words. Primal words. Words of magic and dreams and visions. Words that propel the seeker onward when the winds of the mind blow bitter and cold. Words that strengthen failing resolve when doubt overwhelms the heart and the sense of loss weighs heavily on the soul.

Yearning. Hope. Promise. Salvation.
A pull, a longing, a vague and mysterious force draws the seeker ever onward. Spiritual trials tax their resources. Psychological dangers test their courage. And around each turn of this solitary path? Only the Specter of Loneliness.

Yearning. Hope. Promise. Salvation.
These are the themes of the mythical stories, from *The Iliad* to *The Celestine Prophecy*. These are the words that resonate within the Hero's chest — the driving force of unfulfilled destiny.

Yearning. Hope. Promise. Salvation.
The path is long and arduous, but, like all epic journeys, the rewards are vast and the benefits immeasurable. What follows is the true story of my personal quest for the elusive Grail of Inner Peace — for I, like seekers the world over, was once also drawn...

There is one spectacle grander than the sea, that is the sky; there is one spectacle grander than the sky, that is the interior of the soul.

Victor Hugo

TABLE OF CONTENTS

INTRODUCTION

What is it like inside the mind of an enlightened person? Imagine, upon awaking one morning, you find yourself looking out of the eyes of a Buddha, Dali Lama, Christ or Maharshi.

One of the first things you would notice is just how quiet it is in here. All the reactive thoughts and running commentary are gone. There is an inner silence, a calm stillness, and this amazing sense of expectation. It is much like listening intently to your favorite music when the power suddenly goes out – there is powerful silence, calm stillness and alert awareness. There is this moment and no other.

Because of this stillness, this silence, this lack of mental chatter, your senses are vastly heightened. You see the wonderful play of light and shadows of the morning sun on your bedroom wall; you feel the sheet caress your skin as you roll onto your side; you hear the tiny pauses in the sparrow's song as she sings outside your window.

With a shock, and a bit of disorientation, you realize that this person is – for the lack of a better word – missing. You look into his memory and find his past, his childhood, his yesterdays, but you can't seem to find "him." Like a closed and locked door, you see yourself as very solid, very stable, very real. But when you look for this man, you find a clear, unobstructed doorway. You see where the door was, where the hinges were attached to the frame, but there is no door. Just an opening between the inside world and the outside world.

You experience an intense feeling of potential. This doorway, this emptiness, is very alive. Everything you see or feel comes out of this openness, floats around for awhile, then merges back into it. You see your thoughts arise from it, bounce around a little and then sink back into it. You see your bedroom wall solidify out of it; you see the morning light shine from it; you hear each note of the sparrow's song awaken, tremble, and die back into it. Suddenly you realize a wonderful and profound truth: Nothing equals Nothing equals Everything. Zero grains of sand are equal to zero galaxies. Everything comes from this Emptiness, this great doorway. Everything – including your "self." In a way, you see everything as yourself.

But now you must come back. Back to your solid, separate world. Back to your normal experience of life. You hear the inner noise of constant mental chatter. You feel the tension of stress in your shoulders and neck. You are pulled from the Oneness and return once again to that state of constant anticipation, the world of joy, hope and fears. You return to where everything seems so separate and all emotions feel so personal.

Often you return to that Stillness, but the reoccurring noise in your mind quickly drowns out its subtle whispers. Back and forth between the two realms you go. Back and forth between the Ethereal and the Ego. This constantly fluctuating viewpoint feels very dynamic, very liquid. You no longer feel Solid, like your friends and neighbors, but you know that you are not enlightened like the Ethereal Ones either. What would your life be like, knowing the "truth" of Enlightenment, yet still being stuck with this very ego-centric, self-centered viewpoint?

This is the true story of my journey, from a very Solid, normal person, to a very Liquid, fluid one. I am not enlightened, but I am no longer normal either. It may seem Solid and egotistical to write a book about my own spiritual growth, but this level of awareness is only discussed in complex psychological texts and deep philosophical treaties. It is my hope that by introducing this level of awareness, other spiritual seekers may find some solace knowing that their confusion and doubts are not exclusively their own. That with a little confidence, they can relax their grip on the Solid rock of the ego. Release their grasp and float carefree on the Liquid ocean – an ocean which, on the horizon, merges with the Ethereal sky.

STONE CRACKING

There's no limit to how complicated things can get, on account of one thing always leading to another.

E. B. White

Though I didn't know it at the time, I heard the Siren's song within my mother's womb. Even before I was born, I was being drawn to my death.

All babies are empty vessels, open journals filled with blank pages. Though their stories haven't been written, circumstances have established much of their plots.

Like other children, the values of my parents soon became my own. In ink I'd write each lesson upon a stone, placing it within the empty container of my soul.

Who decides what fills our earthen pots? Who decides our fate? Who writes our moral code? The urn is filled. Fate is sealed. Destiny is written.

The efforts which we make to escape from our destiny only serve to lead us into it.

Ralph Waldo Emerson

Youth – The child's body develops and grows like an acorn to its inevitable fate. The mental lessons of his parents, peers and teachers, effortlessly blend with his own. In his youth, his values, ideals and even his destiny are written in permanent ink on the parchment of his soul. In later years he will try to scratch them out – but ultimately his story is too solid, and the writings resist being erased.

Children have never been very good at listening to their elders, but they have never failed to imitate them.

James Baldwin

From a still and lonely lake, in a wood few people ever go, from the mist a Siren sings a haunting song, "To me. To me. Please come back to me."

Drawn to adventure, to danger, to prove myself a man, I enlisted as a soldier. Upon some of the larger stones inside my urn were the words "Honor" and "Duty" and "Sacrifice."

Muscles grew on bones made strong. "Right" and "Wrong" became crystal clear. "Uphold the American Way" was pounded in my head. "Serve God and Country" was programmed on my Soul.

Under the weight of so many stones, the earthen pot crumbled to dust. What remained was one large and solid rock. On the face, a single character: The capital letter I.

Our virtues are most frequently but vices disguised.

Francois de la Rochefoucauld

Young men lust for many things: For women, for honor, for conquest. He is no different, and he is drawn to adventure like the bee to the flower. The lessons he learns become him. With each passing day, his story grows more solid, his life becomes more defined. No longer is he one with the world, no longer is he carefree. His environment has shaped and formed him. He is a product of his past, a creature of reaction. He is quite simply — a thinking machine.

The chains of habit are too weak to be felt until they are too strong to be broken.

Samuel Johnson

In every life, Fate turns a card, but when, we cannot know. In the barracks one day, she held up a mirror reflecting a darkness deep in my heart.

The mirror hid nothing. The image was clear. The truth undeniable. What I wanted, what I desired, what I lusted to do, was to kill and to maim and to rape.

I guess most people, when their dark side is seen, close their eyes and try to deny it. But the reflection was clear. The facts proven true. Simply put, I was everything I hated.

We often think of our country's enemies as being brainwashed pawns of the State. I looked in my heart and realized the truth: That I was a pawn of the State.

I am always with myself, and it is I who am my tormentor.
Leo Tolstoy

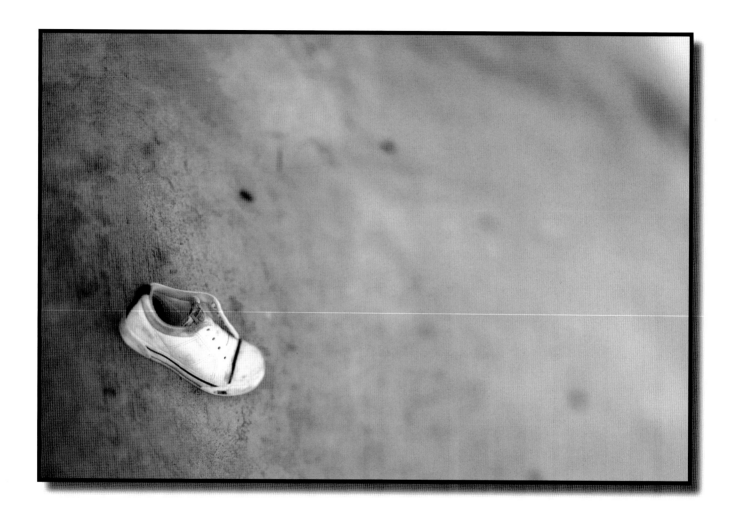

At some point in every young life, innocence is lost — sometimes painfully and brutally. Seeing the darkness within his own soul, causes him to doubt authority. For it is authority that has shaped and formed him. What he held to be true is questioned, and his value system teeters on the edge of a precipice. Suddenly he is alone in a world which seems cold and cruel and heartless. Youth is lost — adulthood begins, and the painful questioning commences.

Every great advance in natural knowledge has involved the absolute rejection of authority.

Thomas Huxley

Who does the hating when you hate yourself? Who is to blame for your actions? The flames of condemnation soon burn out with the waters of deep introspection.

Lost in the woods on a dark moonless night. My compass was broken. My supplies – spoiled. In the shadows, the eyes of the wolves glowed hungrily. Drifting on the wind – the Siren's song.

Beaten and humbled, Death and Truth were my only companions. The trap had been sprung. The battle was lost. All my questions were answered with silence.

Where does one stand when the ground disappears? Where do you turn in the fog? What do you believe in, when you no longer have faith? On the stone, a tiny crack formed.

Man is nothing else but what he makes of himself. Such is the first principle of existentialism.

Jean-Paul Sartre

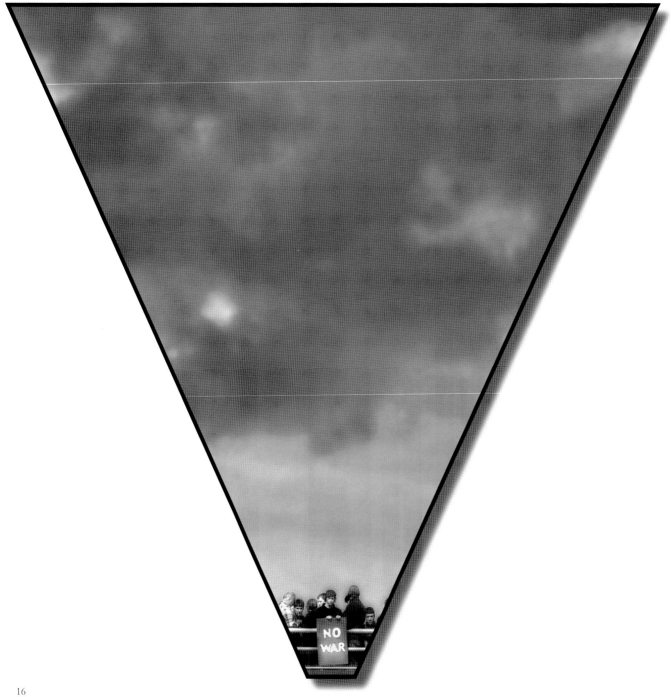

What he was told to be true – was not. What he felt was solid – was unreal. What he believed in – was ultimately proven false. With his first defeat his confidence is shattered. Trauma often precedes change, and a hopeless battle was waged. But a war fought with yourself can never be won. A truce must be called, treaties signed. No one wins, but an uncomfortable peace allows him some rest…

If a house be divided against itself, the house cannot stand.

Mark 3:25

Selfish and motivated, I worked hard at my career. People were used and discarded. A normal, solid life I lived. And the stone of my soul remained solid.

For years I ran the treadmill life. For years I ran and ran and ran. What was bought was broken and bought again. From nagging questions I ran.

I dated many women, but only for a month or two. I made a lot of money, and blew it all away. "I want, I want, I want" – the mantra of the Stone. The mantra of my peers.

Standing alone on a cold, misty morning, I gazed at the freshly turned earth. The flowers were rotting, the clay turned to mud, and at my grandfather's grave, I wept.

Awakening begins when a man realizes that he is going nowhere and does not know where to go.

Georges Gurdjieff

He tries to live a "normal" life, but Life cannot be lived futilely for long. Her nature is to grow, to thrive, to flourish. Once she is awoken, she will not be forgotten again. Here is where he either closes his eyes and turns his back — or he faces the Darkness fully. Past this point, if he is foolish enough to continue forward, he will soon find himself helpless, friendless and alone.

I have called this principle, by which each slight variation, if useful, is preserved, by the term natural selection.

Charles Darwin

Long ago I questioned authority, now I questioned God. What is the Purpose? Why am I here? In the crack on the stone, a crystal of ice formed.

The rational side of my cynical soul, said the questions were not valid. They made assumptions based on beliefs. And beliefs were the hope of the foolish.

From my grandfather's grave, my eyes came to rest on a lone branch filled with new cherry blossoms. Time suddenly ceased. The quiet – profound, and for the first time, I sensed a greater intelligence.

Regardless of what the mind had determined, I could deny the meaning no longer. The ice in the stone shattered the rock into dust. The rain fell and mud formed.

A single event can awaken within us a stranger totally unknown to us.

Antoine de Saint-Exupery

Fresh turned earth with his grandfather deep below; Rotting flowers on the clay; A cherry tree, celebrating Life. The images were burned forever in his mind. He had been wasting his time, filling his life with temporary pleasures, living the unspoken illusion that if he kept busy enough, he would live forever. He had been happily living a lie. A lie he could live no longer.

Death twitches my ear, "Live," he says, "I am coming."

Virgil

MUD SETTLING

We have what we seek. It is there all the time, and if we give it time, it will make itself known to us.

Thomas Merton

In The Tao, the Bible, the Sutras and Koans, answers were sought to questions once vague. To that which all seek, so sought I: the Secrets of Inner Peace.

Within the great wisdom texts, consistent patterns soon arose. The Nature of Man and the Nature of Suffering soon became apparent. Desire was the core of the problem. Selfish desire was the Enemy.

I read many a wise man's thesis, and many a charlatan's too. I listened to the lectures of popular authors. With each, I thought I knew what they knew.

Soon I felt I understood it all. I thought that I was enlightened. To my friends and family, I'd pontificate. All the facts had made me ignorant.

To be proud of knowledge is to be blind with light.
Benjamin Franklin

A little knowledge can sooth the mind, like the proverbial music that sooths the beast. But knowledge is just a mental construct, dependent on a mind. Life arises in many forms, and many of those forms do not have minds. Still, the traveler can now rest for a while, his troubles temporarily vanquished. He can take some time to readjust to his new world, to map out the terrain.

Fill what's empty. Empty what's full. Scratch what itches.

Alice Roosevelt Longworth

Every now and then, I'd catch myself acting in very un-enlightened ways. I hid these actions from my friends. For a long time, I hid them from myself.

I knew the lessons mentally but my actions didn't reflect them. Though I had memorized some foreign phrases, I didn't understand the language.

I had read all the great religious texts, their secrets all quite clear. But the map and the Path are separate things and knowledge is not experience. Though I wanted to be a sage, I was just a fool.

When I compared myself to the Buddha, to Lao Tzu, or the Christ – the truth became apparent: I walked the Path of the Ego and they had walked the Path of the Empty.

Wisdom comes alone through suffering.

Aeschylus

He is faced with a terrible dilemma. Continue on the Path of his Peers, re-
nounce his ways, start a family, be a good boy, and get back on the treadmill
— or turn to the Path of the Seeker, shoulder his pack, say his goodbyes,
and travel across lands that he has so thoroughly mapped yet never visited.
Few ever make it this far, fewer still continue on. The path of true spirituality
requires the seeker to face himself in a way that is both humbling and frightening. To continue on means losing friends, losing respect, and ultimately
losing everything he once thought was solid and true.

The difficulty in life is the choice.

George Moore

I started meditation, I practiced morning, noon and night. Soon again the Siren sang and a few months later I caught a glimpse of the Divine.

For just a single moment, there was this... glimmering. No thought, no mind, no I or It, but a wonderful aliveness just the same. For a fraction of a second, I saw what God must see.

A ray of hope. Required proof. Doubts evaporated and efforts redoubled. As my desire grew, my doom was sealed.

The darkness soon returned, the quiet Stillness lost. Memories, stories and hopes filled my mind, dragging me away from the Truth.

You, yourself, must make the effort. The buddhas are only teachers.

Buddhist proverb

His first glimpse of the Divine. Suddenly he has confirmation. Any stubborn, nagging doubts dissolve and with their death comes a renewed confidence. For until that first glimpse, until that spark of realization is experienced, the seeker must rely on belief, on hope, on the word of others. Unfortunately the experience is short lived and he is returned once again to his solid, ego-based life. He is tenacious though and remembers Saint Peter's dark night. Knowing this is a common experience, he modifies his plans, pulls his cloak around him tight and heads out into the howling gale – the winds of his mind.

Experience, which destroys innocence, also leads one back to it.

James Baldwin

I knew the mind my enemy, but mental knowledge has its place. Over the works of Wilber, Tolle, and Jung I pored. Three very wise men – three very different methods.

Through Carl Jung, I dug down deep into the darkness within my soul. Shadow work and memories repressed. The Unconscious came to light.

Ken Wilber showed in great detail a route to wholeness, growth, and peace. A detailed map, a plotted course, my path now had direction.

And it was through the humble, happy Eckhart Tolle, that I came to see the Truth. A simple, quiet, funny man, a man of ultimate Stillness.

...that is what learning is. You suddenly understand something you've understood all your life, but in a new way.

Doris Lessing

"What is keeping me from the Divine?" This question and this alone is what drives him. It is said that the spiritual seeker must find a guru – that the answers cannot be found without guidance. But who? How do you find one? When you do, how do you know if they are true? So he reads, he studies, and he combines what resonates true with his practice. He meditates, he watches. Blockages become apparent, answers are found, and step by step he walks the path.

He who would learn to fly one day must first learn to stand and walk and run and climb and dance; one cannot fly into flying.

Friedrich Nietzsche

The ego: just a story. The Unconscious: brought to light. The Path forward: well lit. But the mind raged and the Divine remained silent. When Hope flees, Suicide tempts the depressed.

I am not proud of what I did, but this story must stay true. I had lost my glimpse of Eternity and I would do anything to regain it.

When nights never end, when the noise never stills, when the practical becomes the futile – Fear loses its power, desperate actions become feasible, and values are discarded.

On a cool and calm clear night, the full moon reflecting in my backyard pool, I sat on the deck, turned my eyes to the stars, and dropped a hit of acid.

Action is the antidote to despair.

Joan Baez

He was raised as many children are raised — to respect his parents, to stay away from drugs and violence. To treat others with compassion, to follow the laws, to help those in need. And like most children he pushed the boundaries, tested the waters and on his own found the wisdom in the words of his elders. The values became his own and he took them into manhood. But what good are values to a man dying of depression? Where do you go when every door is locked? When the aria of the angels, once heard and cherished, is suddenly silenced?

We know well only what we are deprived of.

Francois Mauria

The light burned my eyes, the air freezing cold, the blanket was coarse and rough. In the nursery, I screamed with the others that day. We wanted to return to the womb.

"Back," I said and back I went. The dark was warm and safe and fluid. But the peace only brief, the contractions very strong and soon my head was crushing.

"Back," I said and suddenly, I felt I was my mother. In the womb there is no Us or Them, just one without an other.

"Back," I said and looking down, I saw my parents coupling. My father soon fell deep asleep, as my mother's sadness drew me toward her.

After your death you will be what you were before your birth.
Arthur Schopenhauer

Under the influence of the drug, he experiences a profound vision of his first moments of life. Never had he thought about how horrible, frightening, and painful life must be to an infant as they are overwhelmed with stimulation. This insight convinces him that the vision is a memory, not something his mind has made up. "Back," he says and each time he travels deeper and deeper into his past.

It is in our idleness, in our dreams, that the submerged truth sometimes comes to the top.

Virginia Woolf

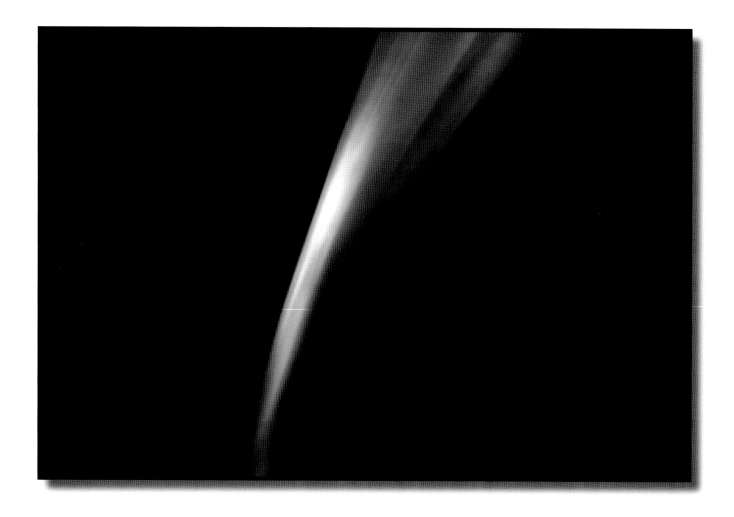

Under the moon on that clear night, both frightened and amazed, I took a deep breath and closed my eyes. "Back," I said, and my whole life changed forever.

Wholeness. Contentment. Joy and Bliss. Awareness without an Other. Love radiating outward into itself. No beginnings, no endings. No births or deaths. To Life, there is no opposite.

From the Stillness, a subtle tug, a tiny ripple on the empty ocean. A single twitch, a little pull and suddenly there were Two.

Ripped apart by desires unknown. She, the World and I, me. No longer One, we now were Two. It's all my fault… Forgive me.

Many men go fishing all of their lives without knowing that it is not fish they are after.

Henry David Thoreau

Like being torn from the womb, this too was a terrible separation, but far, far worse. Because he had failed to learn the lessons of his true Self, a disturbance was created in the Void. With a Big Bang this disturbance created the Universe and he was expelled from Heaven, cast out of Eden, and exiled from his Beloved.

We would often be sorry if our wishes were gratified.

Aesop

Under the moon on that clear night, my tears turned the stars to halos. Wracked with guilt and self-disgust, I had committed the ultimate betrayal.

We had been One, but now no more, my weakness – simple desire. By wanting more, we split in two. I, the Ego and She, the World. I apart from She.

Night and Day divided by Dawn. Forever close but never joined. Two mute lovers just out of reach: destined to see. Doomed never to hear. Doomed never to touch.

What would you do to merge with Her? What atrocities would you commit? What tortures would you endure to be united once again?

If one is lucky, a solitary fantasy can totally transform one million realities.

Maya Angelou

He lay on the ground under the moonlight and through his tears vowed that he would do anything — anything to merge once again with Her. To be One again, he would gladly suffer life and separation and pain and pleasure over and over and over again until he finally mastered his lessons. Until he found the way to join with Her forever.

There are two tragedies in life. One is to lose your heart's desire. The other is to gain it.

George Bernard Shaw

From a still and lonely lake, in a wood few people ever go, from the mist my Siren calls, "To me. To me. Please come back to me."

When the mud settles, the waters clear.

When it is dark enough, you can see the stars.
Charles A. Beard

It was all so suddenly obvious. Amazingly, all the suffering in life made sense. He now saw that after death, we merge back into the One Without an Other. Soon though, our attachments and desires create a conflict, an inner storm. For what is desire, but a lusting for something outside yourself? A lusting that cannot be satisfied in this whole, "Not Two" state. Soon the unity and stillness of the One are torn in half: the "self" and the desired Other. The universe is created, and another lesson must be learned.

Though he doesn't know it yet, from this point on he will live in a twilight world between two realms: the Solid Life of the Ego and the Ethereal Life of the Spirit.

Love says that I am everything. Wisdom says that I am nothing. Between the two my life flows...

Nisargadatta Maharaj

No man remains quite what he was when he recognizes himself.

Thomas Mann

Gradually my perceptions changed. The world had become multi-layered. Everything I saw, I saw two ways – one way Solid, one way Ethereal.

The Solid world we all know well, but the Liquid one is fluid. One moment a tree is just a tree, the next the source of all Life living.

I was no longer normal and yet I knew I wasn't enlightened. I'd still get caught up in the Play, only to remember that my mental Story was just a poem.

Within a year, my Solid friends did flee. They'd shake their heads and cast their judgments. Back on their treadmills they would run to try to catch their phantoms.

Life begins on the other side of despair.

Jean-Paul Sartre

He finds himself in an uncomfortable state. A state somewhere in between enlightened and normal. He starts to think of the normal people as "Solids." Solid because they experience themselves as very real, very important. Their story is who they are. He thinks of the enlightened people as "Ethereals" — those individuals who are no longer attached to the machinations of the mind. People who, in a strange way, seem almost transparent. As for himself and others like him? He takes to calling them "Liquids" — people who flow back and forth between the two extremes. Sometimes caught up in the world of the ego and its importance, sometimes in the world of Divine Emptiness.

The motto should not be: Forgive one another; rather, understand one another.

Emma Goldman

At dawn on the beach on a late autumn morning, as I sat in silent meditation, I felt a tingle cover my skin and my ego shot straight out my head.

Right out the crown I felt it go, and what remained surprised me. For what is left when you drop Yourself? What is left when you are empty?

I looked at the sea and at the sky. I looked at the clouds and seagulls and sand. I saw the same thing everywhere: Stillness within everything – and Stillness is Stillness is Stillness.

When the words are dropped and meanings forgotten, the core of everything is the same. Boundaries fade, the illusion revealed, and the One becomes radiantly apparent.

Learn what you are, and be such.

Pindar

He experiences his first lasting glimpse of the enlightened state. Where the drug of a year before had revealed a possible memory, this experience revealed the Truth of Life. Once all meanings and stories and definitions are dropped – once we see from an unobstructed viewpoint – it becomes blindingly apparent that there is no I or Us or Them. Below all mental symbols, noise and manipulations, there lies only one thing: Awareness. And the Awareness that looks out your eyes, is the same Awareness that looks out your neighbors.

Knowing others is wisdom, knowing yourself is Enlightenment.

Lao-tzu

For half an hour I sat on that beach, grinning like a fool. Though the experience quickly faded, I knew the memory never would. My Solid corpse lay on the rocks as the Siren sang her victory.

Magically my house was sold, the next day all my possessions. I quit my job and life lined up. I let go and I drifted.

I said my goodbyes and drove away. From the Atlantic across to the Pacific. I did not know all the reasons why, but I heard Her call and faithfully followed.

Morning and night I'd meditate. Every day I'd hike the woods. I lived and walked the Spiritual Path, and through my photos I'd save it.

All is change; all yields its place and goes.

Euripides

No longer feeling in synch with the Solid world of his peers — he simply gave it up and walked away. He hoped to find some way to stabilize those mystical glimpses. To get out of this Liquid state that seemed to reside somewhere in the limbo world between that of the Normal and Ethereal people. He escaped to Portland, Oregon, spent much of his time alone, and watched as the grip of his ego loosened.

Solitary trees, if they grow at all, grow strong.

Winston Churchill

Alone I spent my days and nights. Alone I was most often. Of all the deeper levels of Hell, Loneliness must be the darkest.

One day I realized, to my surprise, that my mind had grown quite still. It startled me by how small and distant all my thoughts did feel.

Some nights I'd wake in terrible fear, the doubts and the dread oppressing. When the money runs out, what will I do? Yet Fear felt like a separate entity.

On its own, the mind had calmed and the emotions had become quite distant. Not with trying, just with practice and the ego's grip had gently loosened.

Solitude is the playfield of Satan.

Vladimir Nabokov

His time away from people had a profound affect on his inner life. The meditation and the solitude worked on his consciousness in subtle yet powerful ways. Without trying to force or control the outcome, his mind stilled, his emotions became less personal, and his ego gently softened.

We are used to the actions of human beings, not to their stillness.

V. S. Pritchett

Further I traveled the Ethereal path, not knowing what lay ahead. Though never did I have a guide, I was always mysteriously led.

The traffic lights were always green and parking spaces opened for me. What I needed magically appeared and Her soul was in harmony with me.

It seemed the less there was of me, the more there was of Her. Her song was the breeze flowing through the trees. In my silent mind, her voice I heard.

When life becomes so interconnected, all boundaries lose their meaning. Black and White and Yes and No, no longer are divided.

If you bring forth what is within you, what you bring forth will save you.

Jesus Christ

As his ego weakens, as its grip loosens — his world seems to fill with what can only be described as magic. As the space that was filled with the little self is replaced with Spirit/Life/God the separation between the two fades and a "communication" between them seems to occur. What is needed appears, what is desired transpires and the concepts of self and other seem to merge.

A goose flies by a chart which the Royal Geographical Society could not improve.

Holmes

Eventually, the money ran out and my retreat was forced to come to an end. The time had arrived to bring the lessons back home, to return to the world of the Solids.

Miami is filled with material things, of looks and glamour and status. A Solid, tense, and crowded place, the polar opposite of relaxed, laid back Portland.

But what good is the spiritual search if you only have peace when it's quiet? The true and defining spiritual test, is to experience Stillness during a raging riot.

Upon returning, the trials commenced. Friends and family awakened the ego. From the depths of my newly liquefied soul, the personal Story began to harden.

A man travels the world in search of what he needs and returns home to find it.

George Moore

He returns to his origins, returns to a society so different from whence he came. Though he can't explain all the reasons, he knows this is part of his Quest. In all the great stories and myths of old, the hero must always return to his origins, a magical weapon in hand, a final conflict on the horizon.

He gave the impression that very many cities had rubbed him smooth.

Graham Greene

I found myself in a cubical, writing software for eight miserable hours each day. I'd often catch my mind caught up in some "poor me," self-pitying tale.

But the story was only temporary. Pain is a wonderful reminder. Each stab I felt, was a tap from behind. A tap to awaken and admire.

Back and forth my viewpoint swept. Back and forth between the extremes. Solid and hard. Ethereal and empty. Ripples running across the vast sea.

I soon realized this was alright, to live this fluid, dynamic life. That the Liquid path had vistas as grand as those of the Solid and Ethereal sights.

Sometimes I go about pitying myself, and all the time I am being carried on great winds across the sky.

Ojibway Dream Song

Slowly he starts to become comfortable with this Liquid level of consciousness. He sees it as another lesson, a way of strengthening his awareness of the Ego, thereby reducing its power over him. He may not like this current phase of his outer life, but he knows that, like everything else, it is temporary. Though it may seem obvious, inner peace is only found from within.

If you pursue happiness you'll never find it.

C. P. Snow

A powerful lesson I was destined to learn in mapping out the Liquid level. The Lesson of Love. The Lesson of Lust. The Lesson of the Rock and the Water.

She was so sweet and beautiful too, but she was Solid to her core. I had hoped that our lives could blend and merge, that we could dance to the Song of Amour.

But Solids are very earthly bound, while Liquids want to fly. She wanted the family and traditional life, while all I wanted was oneness with the sky.

She didn't mean to pull me down, but down I came at last. For months I lived the Solid life as the ego's winds froze my Story fast.

Lovers know what they want, but not what they need.
Publilius Syrus

How can love last if the two lovers have different life goals? How can one ask the other to give up their dreams? How can the love of a Liquid and Solid endure? The Solid lover wants to strengthen their attachments to this world, the Liquid to release them. Can love overcome all? Is it possible? They did not know the answers, and so, Love fled.

Love does not consist in gazing at each other, but in looking together in the same direction.

Antoine de Saint-Exuper

MIST LIFTING

I searched through rebellion, drugs, diet, mysticism, religion, intellectualism and much more, only to find that truth is basically simple and feels good, clear and right.

Chick Corea

Sometimes water crashes, sometimes it caresses. When the air is still and the lake is calm, Her whispers can be heard in the darkness.

Water crashes when one cares deeply. The difference between the Real and Imagined creates tension. The mind rages and the waves of suffering grow.

The physical tension reminds me, like a cold slap in the face, and I realize just how blind I am. How much I fight the Present.

Suddenly I'd see the component parts, What Is and What Isn't as pieces of the Whole. Negative and Positive merge together as One – as the Water embraces the Shore.

Love the moment and the energy of the moment will spread beyond all boundaries.

Corita Kent

His experience of life becomes one of acceptance. He understands that sometimes he gets caught up in the world, sometimes he flows with it, and still others he almost disappears, merging into the Ethereal. Desire is not the enemy of the Liquid Life — without desire there would be no change. But it is selfish desire, the desires of the false Ego in conflict with what it experiences as Other that is the source of the friction. This pattern has become apparent to him, not mentally, but physically, and he experiences it as tension — pressure building up inside. He learns to accept this dynamic condition — the constantly varying view of the same thing.

We cannot change anything unless we accept it. Condemnation does not liberate, it oppresses.

Carl Jung

Why do Birds sing in the morning? Why do Cats torment their prey? Why does Man make enemies? The more I looked for the Controller within, the clearer became the pattern.

It became apparent to me, as I tried to understand my actions, that every act I took was based on a simple motivation: Pursue pleasure – flee pain.

But "Pleasure" is not a fixed definition, it varies from moment to moment. Sometimes it is selfish. Sometimes compassionate. But always we experience a benefit.

The more I looked, the more I realized, it is our value system that determines our pleasure. What is important to us, is pleasurable to us. But what is important to each… is different.

Everyone is dragged on by their favorite pleasure.

Virgil

This realization had a profound effect on him. Suddenly control wasn't so important, suddenly trying wasn't so important. Suddenly it became unconscionable to judge his own or others actions. Who is in control? No one. It became obvious that his upbringing, his culture, his conditioning and the circumstances of the moment all determined his actions. What he found pleasurable, what he found important, guided his actions. Suddenly the tension eased, resistance faded and judgment, though tenacious, slowly weakened.

Don't judge any man until you have walked two moons in his moccasins.

Native American saying

Miami is full of people pursuing the Good Life. To look young, to live in freedom, to drive a nice car. To each, these goals are important. If I were in their shoes, I would feel the same.

I desire the Ethereal Life, freedom from the pain of constant wanting. I cannot help what I desire. It is my nature.

When I view the actions of others with this compassionate understanding, a calm overwhelms me, and I feel myself fading toward transparency.

When I look around from this perspective, Life – all Life – becomes at once one and many. The parts all pursue their own form of pleasure, and the One radiates within.

A happy life is one which is in accordance with its own nature.

Marcus Annaeus Seneca

Judgment fades. Appreciation and Gratefulness become a common feeling. Every living creature is doing what is right for itself. Each is fulfilling its destiny. Each is part of the Whole. He is constantly seeing his world from these two perspectives: from the little self, and from the One Self. But they are no longer in conflict, the Liquid viewpoint has been accepted and no longer seems paradoxical. Both viewpoints are right, both are valid, both are true.

As a man is, so he sees.

William Blake

It is strange how the mind works. How you can know a truth, but still act as if you don't. I wonder if it is unconscious? I wonder if it is fear? Sometimes I watch myself do foolish things.

I guess that's who we really are. Just a Watcher looking out. Not trying to do, not trying to be. Just watching our little minds do their little thinking.

I catch myself in judgment of others. Then I naturally react. I watch myself remember. Then I watch as I scold myself. I wonder who all these people are, stuck inside this busy head?

When I remember, I watch. When I forget, I react. When I remember, there is peace. When I forget, I fight a battle I must always lose.

To become the spectator of one's own life is to escape the suffering of life.

Oscar Wilde

Like the tides that naturally cycle between high and low, his awareness cycles between the Ethereal and the Solid. Such is the life of the Liquid. Sometimes Ice, sometimes Mist, but always Water — always in flux — always flowing.

There's never an end for the sea.

Samuel Beckett

Less and less I resist. Less and less I control. Less and less I hold fast to my thoughts, to my memories… to my past. Less and less I feel the need to choose.

Borders disappear when you stand back far enough. Boundaries are only of the mind. Differences between extremes are just opposite ends of a larger whole.

I still get frustrated when asked a dualistic question, "Is this right or wrong?" I don't get frustrated with the question, but with trying to explain my position.

I guess if I were more Ethereal, I'd just flip a coin and give a random answer. But I still get lost in the Solid world. I still get caught up in all the confusion.

The only interesting answers are those which destroy the questions.

Susan Sontag

When he forgets, the ego overtakes him, possesses him like a demon possessing a soul. Still he succumbs to the Solid pull, like gravity pulling the fog to the ground. He knows that dualistic thinking is the result of a limited perspective – of seeing only one side of the Whole. But he knows that this is the nature of life, just as natural as two squirrels who fight for dominance of a branch in a forest filled with empty trees. So silly when viewed from the clouds, yet so vitally important when sitting on the limb.

If the doors of perception were cleansed, everything would appear to man as it is, infinite.

William Blake

Back and forth I go. Back and forth between the two worlds. Over and over and over again. Neither state is permanent.

I know I'm not enlightened. I know I'm no longer normal. Water flows. Life changes and Permanence is an illusion.

I've learned to accept this Liquid state. I've learned to let go of the grasping. Letting go is such a freeing feeling. Letting go, floating, and relaxing.

And how do you let go without conscious control – for conscious control is the ego? You naturally let go of what you don't like. So if you're still clinging, on some level, you want to.

The bird of paradise alights only upon the hand that does not grasp.

John Berry

Letting go. Releasing your grasp. Such a simple act, and yet, it took him so long to let go of trying to control his fate. He likes the idea of the Ethereal, but he also likes the temptations of the Solid. Thus is he destined to live the Liquid life, a world in between the two extremes, between heaven and hell, between normal and enlightened. When he grew weary of fighting the dynamic nature of this level, of the multiple perspectives, of the feelings of being different – when he finally grew tired, his muscles relaxed, his hands unclenched, and he let go of the wave battered rock. He let go and drifted peacefully out to sea.

A true man never frets about his place in the world, but just slides into it by the gravitation of his nature.

Edwin H. Chapin

SUN RISING

The sage stays behind, thus he is ahead. He is detached, thus at one with all.

Lao Tzu

How can I explain the mystical? It seems both magical and quite natural. How can I explain it so the Solids will see? How can I explain the Unknowable?

When I stop the grasping, the controlling, the trying – when my mind is calm and clear – from the Stillness, She appears and all questions and needs are answered.

Of course I have no Solid proof, but indeed I have a theory: When your ego flees, She fills the space, your empty vessel fuller.

When I let go of all the stories, all the fairy tales of who I am, it becomes palpably apparent, that I am much more than just a man.

The essential purpose of the Vedas is to teach you the nature of the imperishable Atman, and to declare with authority, "Thou art That."

Ramana Maharshi

He often experiences the mystical, magical world of a unified existence. The Hindus speak of this level with caution, that the wonderful abilities and experiences can be a trap holding the spiritual seeker enthralled. Because the ego has weakened, the One without an other fills the space of his awareness, much like the air fills a vase that contains a small leak. The water trickles out, and the Ethereal takes its place.

The universe begins to look more like a great thought than like a great machine.

James Jeans

Of course I cannot make it happen, if I try to, She just flees. For it is the ego that so desperately wants, the very ego that blocks its needs.

There is only so much room inside, what it's filled with takes some practice. Either selfish stories of the self, or an Emptiness that is a mystical Fullness.

The paradox is simply this: If you want it you can't have it. Let it go to find what can't be lost. You must let it go in order to gain it.

Who are you behind your busy thoughts? Imagine your story suddenly died. What is left that is looking out your eyes? What are you before the noisy mind?

Explore thyself. Herein are demanded the eye and the nerve.

Henry David Thoreau

He sees the paradox clearly: The more you want it, the less you see it. It is always there, but you don't recognize it if you are too Solid. The Solids want the magical for the power. The Liquids like the magical because it proves their path is true. The Ethereals? Who knows? Maybe they just watch it.

One sees great things from the valley; only small things from the peak.

G. K. Chesterton

When I let go, when I drop it, She appears before me. If I am lucky, I'll have my camera, and She'll take a self-portrait.

I'll see Her in every vein, in every leaf, in every tree. I'll hear Her voice on the wind. I'll feel Her skin in the sheets of the bed. I'll smell Her perfume on the morning air.

As I fade, she appears. As I grow Solid, she flees. I both hate it, and I love it. I want Her, and I want me.

Sometimes I take a breath, and my eyes fill with tears of appreciation.

Men talk about Bible miracles because there is no miracle in their lives. Cease to gnaw that crust. There is ripe fruit over your head.

Henry David Thoreau

Fading, Drifting, Melting — Clinging, Grasping, Holding — Joining, Merging, Blending — Losing, Wanting, Desiring — Dying, Living, Being.

Ever desireless, one can see the mystery. Ever desiring, one can see the manifestations.

Lao Tzu

More and more I catch my mind, in a strangely quiet state. The birds they sing, the clouds they drift, and the trees provide cool shade.

The world, She flows upon Her course, all parts in harmony with all others. Even Man's litter lies naturally in the forest, at home among the flowers.

Man fights his wars, he commits his crimes, he hates, he loves, he preaches. And behind his mind, below his thoughts, She lies still and She watches.

I cannot judge, I cannot blame. Who has control of their nature? Remember who you really are. Remember. Remember. Remember.

Believe there is a greater power silently working all things good, behave yourself and never mind the rest.

Beatrix Potter

Emptiness here is the same as Emptiness there.

The space behind your mind is the same as the space behind mine.

What sees out my eyes, sees out yours.

Walk outside, breath the air…

Walk outside and remember.

The Tao is an empty vessel; it is used, but never filled.

Lao Tzu

QUESTIONS AND ANSWERS

In the beginning you were always talking about doom and doubts and self-loathing. Does the spiritual search have to be so dark?

Self-loathing works as an excellent motivator during the initial stages of the spiritual path. You dislike – or even hate – certain aspects of yourself, so you search for solutions to find some solace. Once you experience a taste of the Divine though, the quest to re-attain such a powerful feeling becomes your motivator. There seems to be only two reasons to do anything, and if you look closely you will see they are based on the same concept. We are either fleeing a painful situation or we are pursuing a more pleasurable one. Big changes in a person's life are often motivated by some horrible event. That event might be as simple as an insight that one is wasting one's life and it's time for a career change, or as traumatic as losing a child to a drunk driver and becoming a spokesperson for MADD. When I hear people complaining about their lives, I often remark to them, "You're complaining because your life isn't bad enough. When it gets bad enough, you'll do something about it."

Wanting to "kill and to maim and to rape" is pretty dark. What was that about?

I was a new recruit in the Army and during basic training, I was really getting into all the shooting, the explosions, and the smell of cordite mixed with the scent of pine needles, sweat, and dirt. Young men are FULL of testosterone and really eat up adventure. The military, in order to be effective, has to basically brainwash you. They can't afford any wimpy, moralistic, liberal types raising their hands during a firefight and asking if they could be excused because they no longer believe that war is justified. I woke up to how effective their brainwashing was when, as punishment for some minor infraction, I was ordered to run through the barracks shouting "KILL! KILL! KILL!" every time my left foot hit the ground. While the entire platoon looked on, I shouted and ran and realized that for the past few weeks, I really did want to kill. My faith in authority was immediately shattered and all the questioning began.

What was the insight you had at your grandfather's grave?

My grandfather had died a week before, but I couldn't attend the funeral. A few days later, I flew up to Pennsylvania to pay my respects. It was a cold, foggy morning, and I stood alone in the empty graveyard staring down on the bare, wet clay. Six feet below lay a man whom I loved dearly. No grass covered the plot; no gravestone had been erected. Flowers were rotting and lying in ruin on the grave, and I couldn't stop my mind from thinking the same thing was happening to his body just below. I was a rather vague agnostic at the time, but when I glanced up and saw the cherry blossoms, covered in dew and so very much alive – the sheer meaning of the coincidence caused me to feel a literal cracking inside. Their Zen-like stillness was both a contrast to the dead flowers at my feet and such a sameness. The balance of it all filled me with an overwhelming feeling of design, a blinding realization that there was some greater, unseen, unifying quality to existence.

Your drug experience seemed to be a turning point in your development. Could you go into that?

First, I'm not advocating drug use, nor am I saying that indulging in them is required to advance along the spiritual path. I was at a brick wall in my development, most likely because I was so rational, and I was seriously contemplating suicide. As a last hope, I researched the usage of hallucinogenic drugs in accounts of other historical spiritual seekers and came to the conclusion that it might just help. With nothing to lose, I had one of my "connected" friends get me some acid. I went home, placed it on my tongue, and tried to meditate.

The experience unveiled answers that I probably already knew on some deeper level. One of the fascinating qualities of LSD is that what you experience, you experience as both real and as an illusion – you know it is a hallucination, and yet, because the visions are so powerfully conscious, you know it contains a truth. To me, the experience was akin to opening a door that had been sealed shut. Suddenly I could see all that I had been missing because of my strict rationality. The drug opened the door, but it took another year before I really started to experience true, waking oneness.

What led up to your satori experience on the beach ("my ego shot straight out my head")?

After the drug experience, my meditation started to deepen. It was almost as if some part of my mind now knew, rather than just theorized, that the ego really wasn't "me." I was (and still am) using these CDs from a company called Centerpointe Research Institute that, when listened to with headphones, slow your brainwaves from the Beta state all the way down to the Delta state – the state that advanced meditators achieve after years and years of practice. I had also discovered Eckhart Tolle, a man I believe to be truly enlightened. Reading his book, *The Power of Now*, attending his lectures, and watching his videos, this – combined with the Centerpointe CDs and meditating at least an hour a day – apparently set my mind up to "let go." It was about a year of this heavy mediation, spiritual reading, and brain wave modification that led up to the satori experience.

Is meditation required to find inner peace?

I don't know, but it sure helps. One of the most powerful lessons you will learn is just how little control you have of the mind. Once you realize that, you start to distance yourself from it. Distancing yourself seems to quiet the mind, almost tame it, so that when you do consciously turn it on to a project, your focus becomes almost laser-like.

At night, I use the Centerpointe CDs while I meditate and often practice a distancing meditation – trying to see "that which is doing the seeing." Sometimes I'll practice the basic – "Counting the Breaths" – to keep my attention "in tune."

I routinely use a sort of mindfulness meditation throughout the day. I watch my mind; I watch my emotions; I watch my unconscious actions. All day long, I'm strengthening my identification with the Witness, while naturally weakening my attachment to the ego. Nonetheless, since I'm not enlightened, I still (quite often) get caught up in the mind/ego story. That's why I'm always practicing.

What do you mean by the "ego as just a story"?

I first came across this concept when I was reading Ken Wilber. In most of his books, he will talk the reader through his "pointing out" instructions. He received those from Ramana Maharshi, a well respected and enlightened individual who, unfortunately, is no longer with us. Basically Wilber points out that if you can see something, it isn't you. It can't be you because you are doing the seeing and it is something else being seen. So you sit down and try to see who is doing the seeing. You sit down and try to see yourself. Pretty soon, you realize that everything you know about yourself, you can see – "I'm a man, I write books, I'm a photographer" – and that all this "stuff" is just a story about yourself and not that which is doing the seeing.

I then came across Eckhart Tolle, and using an entirely different vocabulary and speaking from his own experiences (which are vastly different from Wilber's), he says practically the same thing. Tolle, in his lectures, is always (I think unconsciously) moving his hand about in front of his eyes when he talks about his "story" of himself. He does the same thing when he talks about his mind and thoughts. For him, it is literally out there in front of him. He's not that story; it is something that he experiences. It is really very cool to see him talk. You can order his videos off his website – I highly recommend them.

Do you have to escape from the world, as you did, to find inner peace?

I doubt it. I'm a pretty introverted kind of man, so escape was the most comfortable and natural method for me to get really serious about my quest. If your nature is more social, a student/teacher method might be more appropriate. We all need guidance though, be it from books, teachers, or even serious attention to world events. I do think that alone time (not necessarily as drastic as a year long retreat) for deep and honest introspection is required though.

Why do you refer to "God" in the feminine?

During my drug experience, I was torn apart from what Rumi would call, my Beloved. Before this separation, I/We were One and everything was I/Us. This vision left me with the undeniable feeling that I had been forced to take the form of a man (to learn my lessons), and she was forced to take the side of everything else – everything in the universe that was not me. Being a heterosexual male, I naturally felt that my other half was feminine. As rational as I am, some primal, mystical part of me still feels that She is everything and I am just this lowly human. It feels good to feel this way, like I am not alone in the world, so I don't try to dissuade myself of this feeling.

Is love between a Solid and a Liquid possible?

I don't know. Never ask a fat man about diet advice, and never ask a single man about relationship advice.

You don't really see light glowing in trees do you?

When I say "a cute puppy," do you see a cute puppy? Yes and No. You definitely see something, it just isn't physical. When I have my camera with me, and I'm in the "zone," everything – everything – is full of that light. Look at any photo in this book; try to see what I was seeing when I released the shutter. Can you see the Unity? Can you see that all-pervading Light?

Are you serious that you don't think people are in control of themselves?

Scary thought, I know. The illusion of self-control is a strong one. Still, if you look closely at any of your past actions, you'll find that the motivation for those actions was always the same: Pursue pleasure or flee pain.

What is the key to inner peace for a Liquid?

Realizing that you've come a long way from your old, Solid self. Realizing that you've traveled far, and it is time to take a break. Once you see how tightly you've been clinging to this ideal of Enlightenment, how Enlightenment is just another goal that the ego is trying to attain (I'll be happy when I'm Enlightened!), you start to become comfortable with the dynamic, flowing nature of the Liquid. Yeah, sometimes I get angry in traffic. Sometimes I'll catch myself feeling self-conscious. So what? I'm not enlightened. But the cool part is, the less you beat yourself up for acting "un-enlightened," the easier it becomes to stay as the Witness. Strangely enough, you have to let go of the Grail in order to drink from it.

Can't I just think my way through to Enlightenment?

You have to get past thoughts. Numerous psychologists refer to the higher levels of conscious development as Post-Rational. "Thinking your way through" is just another example of how the mind sucks you into identifying with your thoughts rather than experiencing your thoughts. When you experience your thoughts, you are identifying with the Witness. It is important to understand the word "identifying." It means "you experience yourself as." Most people experience themselves as their thoughts, not as what is watching their thoughts.

So can you think your way through to Enlightenment? No. You must see who is doing the thinking. And if you can see yourself, then you are doing it wrong.

RESOURCES

If you would like to explore the field of inner growth further, either through rational or experiential methods, you may find the following information useful.

Centerpointe Research Institute – http://www.centerpointe.com

This company makes the audio CD's that I refer to in the Question and Answers section. Used with headphones, they greatly affect the "depth" of your meditation. Free to try.

Debbie Ford – http://www.debbieford.com

Shadow work (becoming aware of your repressed unconsciousness) can dramatically speed up your progress on the spiritual path. The father of the shadow is, of course, Carl Gustav Jung, but for a more readily accessible teacher, not to mention easier to understand, I whole-heartedly recommend the work of Debbie Ford and her *The Dark Side of the Light Chasers*.

Eckhart Tolle – http://www.eckharttolle.com

Amazing man. Simple, yet profound. The easy to read *Power of Now* will either put you to sleep if you are not ready for his teachings, or it will literally wake you up. I highly recommend his videos which can be ordered from his website.

Ken Wilber – http://wilber.shambhala.com

For the serious seeker. This man has been called, and rightly so, the Einstein of Human Consciousness. For an excellent introduction to his work, see *A Theory of Everything*.

Spiral Dynamics – http://www.spiraldynamics.org

A fascinating and easy to grasp mapping of human consciousness development. Many developmental psychologists have adopted this model in defining different levels of human evolution. Very useful in pin-pointing "where you are" and what the next level looks like.

Fading Toward Enlightenment – http://FadingTowardEnlightenment.com
Latest news and updates on this book and the author.

Wayne Wirs – http://waynewirs.com
The author's personal site.

AFTERWORD

For the past six months, I have been a business man. Having decided that I wasn't going to be held back any more, I gave up trying to go the traditional publishing route. On a credit card and a prayer, I started my own publishing company - Missing Man Press. In doing so, I gave up all excuses. I threw everything I had into making *Fading Toward Enlightenment* the absolute best I could. I gave it my all. If it fails, there will be no one to blame but myself.

What I didn't expect, though, was that I would lose sight of *Her*. For six months, I have been researching book manufacturers and learning about distributors, discount schedules, paper weights, and opacities. All the things that a publisher of books needs to know. Marketing plans, trade reviewers, publicity strategies. All this rational stuff. All this noise. All this, excuse the pun, Solid crap.

New Years Day, 2005. The book is sitting on my hard drive ready to go to the printer. The end of Phase I of my extended 15 minutes of fame, and all I can think about is how much I hate being a publisher, how much I hate all the business planning and anal "rules" of getting a book reviewed and into the stores.

New Years Day, 2005. Over a hundred thousand people dead in southern Asia and eastern Africa from a wall of water born of an earthquake on the ocean floor. Millions left homeless, penniless, and mourning their lost loved ones. One of the greatest relief efforts the world has ever seen, assisted by hundreds of nations, and I'm worrying about font sizes and image quality.

New Years Day, 2005. I'm sitting at my desk, watching the news, when suddenly *She* whacks me on my head. *She* points to the television; *She* points to my book, and *She* tells me that I need to remember *Her*, to bring *Her* back into my life, my game plan, my future.

New Years Day, 2005. The price for *Fading Toward Enlightenment* had already been set to $24.95. Twenty-five bucks is a little on the high side for an inspirational book, but is on the low side for an art book. The price was right. It would leave me the necessary room to make a profit after printing costs and the discounts to distributors. It was right in line with the marketplace. Then *She* called, and, as always, I had to follow. I wrote *Fading Toward Enlightenment* to help the seekers of the world find inner peace. But *She* wanted more. "Not everyone is a seeker," *She* reminded me as my mind stilled, "but everyone suffers." Some suffer a lot.

Time to live True. Time to get off my butt. Time to make a difference.

Because of the pricing structure, I can't do anything about books sold through the normal distribution channels: bookstores, Amazon, or specialty shops. But, I can do something about books I sell on my own. So, for the suffering of this world, I make this pledge:

For each copy of this edition purchased through the website, FadingTowardEnlightenment.com, I will donate $5.00 to the charity of the customer's choice.

This is straight out of my pocket, straight out of my business and marketing plan. My financially responsible father is going to kill me. MBA's are going to roll their eyes, and my creditors are going to start legal action. Frankly though, I don't expect them to understand. I DO expect *you* to. Five dollars. Not a percentage of profits. Not a vague and mysterious amount. Five bucks. *Fading Toward Enlightenment* was written to help the Seekers with their inner suffering. Now Seekers in return - by purchasing this book directly on the website - can help others who suffer, suffer a little less.

In many parts of the world, five dollars can save a life. If you like this book, tell people. The power of Word of Mouth should never be underestimated. In the Indian Ocean, a tragic tidal wave inspired this crusade. Maybe, with your help, we can start a tidal wave of our own - one that heals rather than destroys. Go to FadingTowardEnlightenment.com. Buy a book and help ease the suffering.

Peace.

Wayne Wirs
January 4, 2005
Coconut Grove, FL

St. Louis Community College
at Meramec
LIBRARY